World Book, Inc.
180 North LaSalle Street
Suite 900
Chicago, Illinois 60601
USA

For information about other "True or False?" titles, as
well as other World Book print and digital publications,
please go to www.worldbook.com.

For information about other World Book publications,
call 1-800-WORLDBK (967-5325).

For information about sales to schools and libraries,
call 1-800-975-3250 (United States) or 1-800-837-5365
(Canada).

Library of Congress Cataloging-in-Publication Data for
this volume has been applied for.

True or False?
ISBN: 978-0-7166-3725-7 (set, hc.)

The Ancient World
ISBN: 978-0-7166-3726-4 (hc.)

Also available as:
ISBN: 978-0-7166-3736-3 (e-book)

Printed in China by Shenzhen Wing King Tong Paper
Products Co., Ltd., Shenzhen, Guangdong
1st printing July 2018

Staff

Executive Committee

President
Jim O'Rourke

Vice President and
Editor in Chief
Paul A. Kobasa

Vice President, Finance
Donald D. Keller

Vice President, Marketing
Jean Lin

Vice President, International
Maksim Rutenberg

Vice President, Technology
Jason Dole

Director, Human Resources
Bev Ecker

Editorial

Director, New Print
Tom Evans

Writers
Grace Guibert
Mellonee Carrigan

Managing Editor
Jeff De La Rosa

Librarian
S. Thomas Richardson

Manager, Contracts and
Compliance
(Rights and Permissions)
Loranne K. Shields

Manager, Indexing Services
David Pofelski

Digital

Director, Digital Product
Development
Erika Meller

Digital Product Manager
Jonathan Wills

Manufacturing/Production

Manufacturing Manager
Anne Fritzinger

Production Specialist
Curley Hunter

Proofreader
Nathalie Strassheim

Graphics and Design

Senior Art Director
Tom Evans

Senior Visual
Communications Designer
Melanie Bender

Senior Designer
Isaiah Sheppard

Media Editor
Rosalia Bledsoe

TRUE OR FALSE?

THE ANCIENT WORLD

WORLD BOOK

www.worldbook.com

TRUE OR FALSE?

Things more than 100 years old are ancient.

FALSE!

Ancient refers to things and people from thousands of years ago. When we talk about ancient civilizations *(SIHV uh luh ZAY shuhns)*, we mean groups of people and the places where they lived from about 3000 B.C. until around 500 A.D. That means from 1,500 to 5,000 years ago!

7

The Roman Empire fell apart because it was too big.

An empire is a group of nations under one government. It might seem like a big empire would be a strong empire. But the Roman Empire grew too big to govern! It covered so much land that it was hard to keep invaders out. It collapsed in 476 A.D.

Ancient China was ruled by people who belonged to powerful families.

14

These people started what are called dynasties. A dynasty is a series of rulers who belong to the same family. The first Chinese dynasty that we know about is the Shang dynasty, whose rule began around 1766 B.C., almost 3,800 years ago.

All of the Seven Wonders of the Ancient World are still around today.

Pyramids of Egypt at Giza

Hanging Gardens of Babylon

Temple of Artemis at Ephesus

Lighthouse of Alexandria

Statue of Zeus at Olympia

Mausoleum at Halicarnassus

Colossus of Rhodes

17

The Seven Wonders of the Ancient World were things built thousands of years ago. Wars, fires, and earthquakes have destroyed six of them. Only the pyramids of Giza in Egypt are still standing.

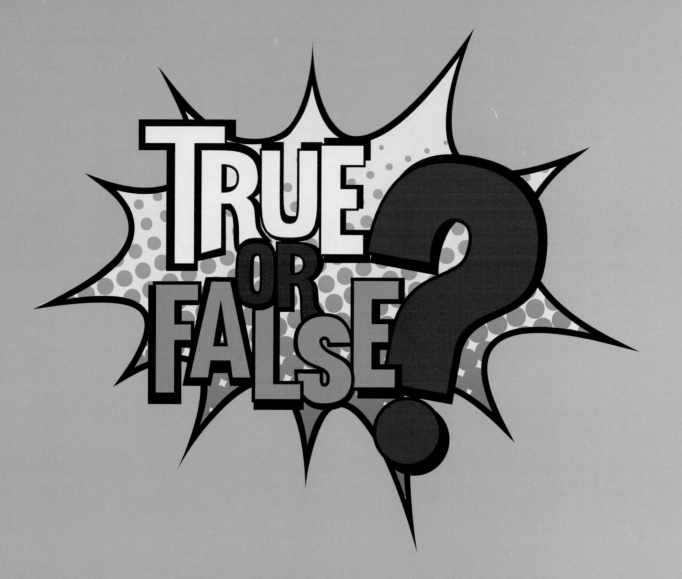

The ancient Greeks had funny beliefs about food.

Food was important to ancient
Greek people. Some ancient Greeks
thought that spirits of people that
had died ended up in beans!

All mummies are from ancient Egypt.

FALSE!

The ancient Egyptians are famous for mummifying *(MUHM uh fy ing)* the bodies of important people, such as their kings. Mummification is preparing a dead body so it doesn't rot.

But the ancient Egyptians weren't the only people to mummify their dead. The ancient Chinese, the ancient Inca of South America, the Ancestral Pueblo people of the American Southwest, and other ancient cultures all made mummies.

TRUE OR FALSE?

Famous Roman general and political leader Julius Caesar was murdered by his friends.

TRUE!

Caesar was stabbed by other men who governed Rome with him. They were afraid he was going to make himself king!

The Great Wall of China can be
seen from the moon.

From that far away, the Great Wall blends into the land around it. Trying to see the Great Wall of China from the moon would be like trying to see a single human hair from 2 miles (3 kilometers) away!

All gladiators *(GLAD ee ay tuhrz)* were men.

Gladiators were trained warriors who fought battles to entertain the ancient Romans. Most gladiators were prisoners of war, slaves, or criminals. But sometimes, soldiers, politicians, and even women fought!

TRUE OR FALSE?

Ancient Egypt was nicknamed "the gift of the Nile."

TRUE!

The Nile River flows through Egypt. Every year during ancient times, it overflowed. This made the soil along the Nile rich for farming. Farmers could grow huge amounts of food.

The Nile was also the main transportation route. An ancient Greek historian named Herodotus *(hih ROD uh tuhs)* called Egypt "the gift of the Nile" for all these reasons.

**The Olympic Games began
in ancient Greece.**

The Olympic Games began in a Greek
city called Olympia in the 1200's B.C.
Only men could compete in the games.

TRUE OR FALSE?

Ancient Roman men wore
togas all the time.

A toga was a large piece of cloth which was wrapped loosely around a person. Togas were worn only by grown-up men and mostly only on special occasions. For everyday, Roman men wore other clothing, such as the tunic *(TOO nihk)*. The tunic was a gown that hung to the knees or below.

Gladiator fights were the most popular entertainment in ancient Rome.

Gladiator fights drew huge crowds. The fights happened in the Colosseum, which could probably fit about 50,000 people. But the most popular form of entertainment was chariot racing! Chariot races took place in the Circus Maximus, a track and stadium that could hold about 250,000 people!

55

Sometimes, when making a mummy, the ancient Egyptian worker pulled the dead person's brains out through his or her nose!

TRUE!

Egyptians were careful with some of the internal organs in a dead body when they were mummifying it. The ancient Egyptians thought the brain was not important. When a body was being mummified, usually a hook was stuck up the nose. The brain was pulled out...and tossed out!

TRUE OR FALSE?

Ancient people didn't wear makeup.

FALSE!

The earliest makeup we know of was used by ancient Egyptians and Greeks.

63

Some ancient buildings are still used today.

65

It might seem like things that are so old could not be useful today, but that is not so. Some things made in ancient times were really advanced! Many ancient Roman bridges are still standing more than 2,000 years after they were built, and a few are still in use today.

The pyramids have kept Egyptian kings' riches safe for thousands of years.

Thieves broke into most of the pyramids, stole the gold, and sometimes destroyed the mummies. Later on, Egyptian kings stopped using pyramids and built secret tombs deep in cliffs.

The Chinese have used chopsticks for thousands of years.

Chopsticks were invented before the ancient Shang dynasty even began. They may have been around since as many as 9,000 years ago!

Caligula *(kuh LIHG yuh luh)*, an ancient Roman emperor, made his horse a government official!

76

TRUE!

Caligula's favorite horse was named
Incitatus *(in KIH tuh tuhs)*. That
word means "swift" or "speedy"
in Latin. Some old stories tell that
Caligula made him a senator!

Ancient Egyptians hated cats.

Cats were sacred (holy) to ancient
Egyptians. Most families had a
pet cat to bring them luck!

There were real dragons
in ancient China.

FALSE!

Dragons are imaginary creatures. But the idea of them was very important to the ancient Chinese. Dragons represented the rulers and their power. A lot of dragons appear in ancient Chinese art!

The first plays came from
ancient Greece.

Ancient Greeks liked to go to the theater and see a show! You can see the ruins of some ancient theaters still today.

DID YOU KNOW...

Legend says that **Rome was founded** by twin boys, Romulus and Remus, who were **raised by a wolf**.

Some people in ancient Egypt kept **crocodiles** as pets!

Apples were **symbols of love** in ancient Greece. Throwing one at a person showed that you liked them!

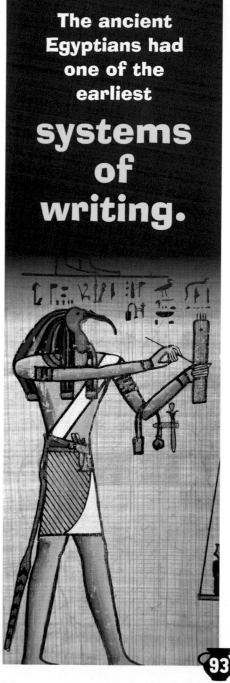

Greeks have been making and eating **feta cheese** since ancient times.

Ancient Romans used to **lie down on couches** at the dinner table.

Index

A

"ancient," meaning of, 4–7
apples as symbols of love, 93

B

brains in mummies, 56–59
bridges of ancient Rome, 66–67
buildings, ancient, still in use, 64–67

C

Caesar, Julius, 28–31
Caligula, 76–79
cats in ancient Egypt, 80–83
chariot races, 54, 55
China, ancient
   chopsticks in, 72–75
   dragons in, 84–87
   Great Wall of, 32–35
   mummies of, 27
   rule by families, 12–15
chopsticks, 72–75
Circus Maximus, 54
Colosseum, 54
Colossus of Rhodes, 17
crocodiles, 92

D

dragons in ancient China, 84–87
dynasties, Chinese, 15

E

Egypt, ancient
   as "gift of the Nile," 40–43
   cats in, 80–83
   crocodiles as pets in, 92
   makeup in, 61–63
   mummies of, 24–27, 56–59, 70
   pyramids of, 17–19, 68–71
   writing system in, 93

F

feta cheese, 93
food, 21–23, 93

G

gladiators
   female, 36–39
   popularity of fights by, 52–55
Great Wall of China, 32–35
Greece, ancient
   first plays in, 88–91
   food in, 21–23, 93
   Herodotus of, 43
   makeup in, 62
   Olympic Games in, 44–47

H

Hanging Gardens of Babylon, 17
Herodotus, 43

I

Inca, 27
Incitatus, 78

L

Lighthouse of Alexandria, 17

M

makeup, 60–63
Mausoleum at Halicarnassus, 17
moon, 32–35
mummies
   destruction of, 70
   other than Egyptian, 24–27
   removal of brains from, 56–59
mummification, 26–27, 58

N

Nile River, 40–43

O

Olympia, Greece, 17, 47
Olympic Games, 44–47

P

plays in ancient Greece, 88–91
Pueblo people, ancestral, 27
pyramids of Egypt
   as wonder of the world, 17–19
   safety of riches within, 68–71

R

Rome, ancient
   bridges of, 66–67
   Caligula's horse in, 76–79
   fall of empire, 8–11
   gladiators in, 36–39, 52–55
   lying down for meals in, 93
   murder of Julius Caesar in, 28–31
   Romulus and Remus legend of, 92
   togas on men in, 48–51
Romulus and Remus, 92

S

Seven Wonders of the Ancient World,
   16–19
Shang dynasty, 15, 75

T

Temple of Artemis at Ephesus, 17
theaters, 91
togas, 48–51
tunics, 50

W

women as gladiators, 36–39
writing system of ancient Egypt, 93

Z

Zeus statue at Olympia, 17

Acknowledgments

Cover: © Nataleana/Shutterstock; © Luis Louro, Shutterstock; © Miha De, Shutterstock

4-93 © Shutterstock